Noemi
&
Lips of Sweetness

ALSO BY AHMAD AL-KHATAT

The Bleeding Heart Poet
Gas Chamber
Love on the War's Frontline
Wounds from Iraq
Roofs of Dreams
The Grey Revolution

Noemi
&
Lips of Sweetness

**poems by
Ahmad Al-Khatat**

Poetic Justice Books
Port St. Lucie, Florida

©2020 Ahmad Al-Khatat

book design and layout: SpiNDec, Port Saint Lucie, FL
cover image: Ilian Flores Ldt

All rights reserved.

No part of this book may be used or reproduced in any manner whatsoever without written permission except in the case of brief quotations embodied in critical articles and reviews. Members of educational institutions and organizations wishing to photocopy any of the work for classroom use, or authors, artists and publishers who would like to obtain permission for any material in the work, should contact the publisher.

Published by Poetic Justice Books
Port Saint Lucie, Florida
www.poeticjusticebooks.com

ISBN: 978-1-950433-53-7

FIRST EDITION
10 9 8 7 6 5 4 3 2 1

*For Ann, Mona, and Noemi.
Thank you for always being there for me.*

contents

One Magical Kiss	3
A Little Love	4
Lips of Sweetness	5
Every Move You Make	6
Little Secret	7
Be My Shahrazad	8
You Are Love	9
Let Love Grow	10
The Age of Love	11
Noemi	12
Painting You	14
The Sea Waves	15
I Just Want Your Love	16
A Side of Heaven	18
My Beloved Is	19
Cold Hands	22
My Angel	23
A Leaf to Your Branch…	24
Sleep Well	25
We Are One…	26
out of	28
God's Whiskey	29
Lips of an Angel	30
After Twelve in the Morning	31
Your Lips Are Mine	32
Above Your Lips	33
haiku	35

Noemi
&
Lips of Sweetness

One Magical Kiss

It is the perfect time to
kiss me in the moment
rest your lips on mine
pulling at my tongue like a lollipop

Feel free to kiss me more
than once, twice, until I get
a taste of your pure love
that grows lively and profound

without your love and support
I would be a guest by the door.
Your kindness below the moonlight
steals my breath and gives me chills

before you, every other cuddle
I had in my past had been wrong,
Now, the universe has turned into spring,
as I watch the flowers bloom for you

I inhale your expensive perfume, and
I become numb when I get a loving taste,
I enjoy smelling your body's scent,
resting on my mind from the noise of war

The candles denied my wishes
since no one sent wishes for me.
with eyes crying I wished myself
to see the sunshine on your face

when I miss you, I cannot dream
of you, when you are sleeping
in my heart you are the warmth and solace
will you come back before I sleep by myself?

Ahmad Al-Khatat

A Little Love

Away from the blowing leaves
near the pages of a romantic novel,
by the end of the last chapter,
I have a little love for you

I will write about it below the sunshine
on the passionate sheets of the warm night
while your love stirs everywhere I miss,
I inhale your scent and dance with you alone

We are meant to be together, even if
love will be a war, without a doubt I will protect
you until I die away from your watery
eyes, therefore you will be smiling at my funeral

The man who fell in love with the moon
was me, and as I was like the rain falling down
still unable to create a river to make you
happy, but your beauty has always been a gifted sight

Every love letter from your sweet mouth,
are written on my bones and tattooed on
my spirit, so I can show you that I will be yours forever
even my coffin will be coloured of your forgiveness

All I have learned from love, is yours
deserves a bouquet of flowers that whispers
about my love in my blood, it is a scent of that
drifts up toward the stars, that witnessed our first moves

Lips of Sweetness

Your sweet lips speak nothing but kind words,
as if you were reading verses from heaven,
when those lips draw near me in bed
I hear the echoes of lovers from the distance moon

Your eyes and lips are the first ones to remind
me of my desires on the lake under the stars and moon
At night I enjoy the rain because it spreads
your taste upon your skin below your red dress

The universe has moody seasons, with
people who whisper to break our shields
but come closer to me and my secrets will
become the shadow to protect you all night

For you, I will drink your wine
and break all the bottles of sorrow
For you, I will inhale your scent
and damages all my grieves

Even your perfume has a promise
to seek you with the beats of my heart
hopefully, I will turn myself into a
candle to hear your voiceless wishes

Every Move You Make

Every move you make with me
I feel the wind blowing my soul
to you with a scent of love to your
port to take you above the rooves of loneliness

Before the night you are dripping
honey, and in the daytime I am
drinking honey, of your flowery lips
with tears to asking you to come back

I will tell you that you are my mirror
as we cry together and I laugh my own
because your body and red lips are
the reason why I can see the stars

Little Secret

Do you want to know a secret
I adore your dancing in the dark
With my eyes closed, I smile with tears

Only a kiss would end my thirst
to write haikus, and free verse,
with birds singing love songs
Hope can be easy to
wish or dream with you
but Baghdad has destroyed my infancy hopes

O Noemi stay with me a bit longer
Across the line, enter my soul and
tell my spirit that everything will be
Alright...

Ahmad Al-Khatat

Be My Shahrazad*

I need space above the skies
To show you how much I evolved
In loving you from a rainbow
As once I was the dullest rain in the desert

Finding our way home is no
Longer, out of the question your
Heart is the most beautiful country,
as it requires love and not a nationalist

Holding our two trusted hands together
As we walk across the broken bridges,
It could lead my vision to a dream,
to break the world's boundaries

Since we belong to this toxic earth
We are cursed to death for no reason.
Our days are hot as fire, and as cold as ice
Therefore, stay strong as the mountains

In the shadow of beautiful darkness
We are not the strangers to undress,
With every breath you take from me
A flower in heaven blooms of your scent

Be my Shahrazad, and kiss my lips
Before the wind blows with red roses,
All over your nude body to hide you
From my joyfulness and pleasure

*Shahrazad is a legendary Persian queen who is a storyteller in the book of *One Thousand and One Nights*, who told the king stories with meaningful lessons to avoid her death.

You Are Love

I am collecting pieces of love
Beneath the branches of love
By the colourful leaves of love
next to the aged love roots
To build a nest of love

My blood is flooding love
My wine is red love
My heart beats for love
My voiceless crush is love
My garden is full of love roses

The doves will sing about love
The moon will wear a love necklace
And I will write about spring and love
Only because you are love
Enlighten me and turn me into love

I enjoy the dessert of love strawberries
To dream of her shadow of love
Only because she is the queen of love
God inspired her flesh from colours of love
as her voice still plays love in my desert

Let Love Grow

Did you know that having you in my
Life, heart, and mind I am healthier since
my days are nothing but sunny and light

The night fell and I am busy thinking of you
as you will be counting the stars in the north
And make my worries go away with a kiss

Your lips are the taste of my affection
Your eyes are the rain of my temptation
Therefore, rest well and let love grow

If you stand by the flowered garden
Flowers and roses will breath of your
Scent only because you are an angel

With pink chains, silk ribbons, and
Fine threads. I will tie myself down
Waiting to be released to you

The Age Of Love

Today, the universe celebrates the birthday
Of my only gifted, princess, and my fiancée.
The clouds will turn transparent like my heart
And blue like the night above the birthday candles

You are the chosen sin from the god of desires
You are the hottest wave from the sea of saltness
Take me to a homeland of nobody's words that matter
And revive my skin to melt a thousand times

With an emotional ribbon tying my spirit down to a pillow,
I unchain your feelings from the blanket
Therefore, nothing will be personnel or private
Love doesn't have a uniform but a lusty scent

By any other name should I write on your cake
Two days, and already it seems like twenty years
That we were friends since the night you were
Born to be my past, present, and future

No more secrets nor stories to hide,
In my hands, there is your name, whenever I
Read it, tears fall on my cheeks like the rain
When it falls on the window of a lonely widow

Train me to be the age of love like yours today
Standing up and looking for paradise full of
Jasmines and red roses, blooming only for the
Taste of your honey lips and strawberry nipples

Behind the old trees shadows in the north
I would intentionally break my muscles for you
Healing from you is worth to extend into a lifetime
I love you darling, and happy birthday again

Noemi

Noemi,
Let us together swear in this life,
That we will keep our love true
See me, feel me, and judge me
Just do not hurt me from my tears

In one week, we have seven days
and there is not a day that
I cannot stop missing you,
And dream of your complexion.
we were once love birds
Drifting with joy that gives us
Wings to fly by the beautiful nest

You are the happiness to my life
You are the hope to my success,
What should I say when you smile
And I get thirsty as a dying solider

When the moon will be yours forever
Do not leave me by the jealous stars
When my heart will be yours forever
Do not stop it from healing after my
Death

Did you know that when I make you
Cry with tears rolling down your cheeks
I see the map of death forcing me to
Go and walk with two bleeding hands?

Noemi, help me bury the darkness
And let our love create the spring
Where I can feel your kissing lips
faraway in my moonlit bedroom

God will protect you from nightmares
And I will love you like a mother cares
for her only child, I will draw for
You a ring and ask you romantic question

Will you marry me Noemi? No pressure
If it is yes, then unwrap me from anxiety
And if it is no, tie me down mercilessly to
The point I will never close my eyes without
Saying your name before I die.

Ahmad Al-Khatat

Painting You

I will be painting you below
the curious moon next to
a pallet of mixed emotions
with a brush full of memories

The truth is I am a sad tear
and not a colour of the rainbow
in your eyes all the colours
dance over your canvas

I see the smile of yours truly
and the arrival of the summer
sunrise and a feeling thirst
of your lips under the rain

Make me your model for a moment,
catch me with your will for an hour
my soul and eyes must be awake
to feel your touch like an angel's kiss

I will colour your moist
lips with a colourful leaf from autumn
in your hair and I will draw the running
horses dancing around your scent forever

The Sea Waves

Here I am a lucky man
Seeking for a heaven
By the sea waves

Hearing your echo
Hearing your whispers
Hearing your tales

When you are next to me
thinking and wondering
Where love will lead us

You hold my hand tightly
And I smile for you
And I weep for myself

You offer me a little kiss
And I understand
You are the life I die for

I Just Want Your Love (Noemi)

We all ask for many things
Some objects fade away while
Others survive but as long as I live
You are the only woman I need

My first kiss with you was magical
I could taste your lips and
together we said welcome to the
Blue moon and goodbye to the sun

Never think about being alone
Never wish for anything else
I just want your love for the rest of
My journey away from tears

My first year with you is more than
A dream I could have asked for
I am honoured to be the man who adores
The seasons by you as an inspiration

Light the candles and fly by the stars
And let me be a vampire biting your
bloodless flesh and nonexistent pain,
Instead I will tattoo my love for you

Noemi & Lips of Sweetness

Noemi, you are the one that taught me how
To live and dream immensely, away from
my dark fantasies of death with a knife
Next to my tears in the lonesome nights

I am numb under your fingers, guiding me
while I melt from you on top of my lusty
Earthquake that will make us into two stones
Catching friendly fire in the middle of every night

I just want your love and nothing else matters
If you are thirsty drink the water from my spirit's scent
And dance with me in Baghdad before the tears
Of joys become black like in the day of my funeral

Your strawberry bites are still moist from my smile
And your perfume is still alive on my neck and beard
If someone comes and tries to break us apart,
I would blind him from how much I miss you right now

Ahmad Al-Khatat

A Side of Heaven

The night I confessed to my darling Noemi
I found out that my pure emotions were
Never a forbidden wine to drink with pleasure
And getting drunk with her love

The moon has been friendly with the stars
But why are my tears woken by the sleeping clouds
As she stayed far when I needed her to wipe
The fog to let the rain wash my burning path

I did not want to weep, but my misery of the past
Blinded me from my pathway into her open arms
I kept no secrets from the observes who forced
Me to take an old and dirty road that ends with joy

I spoke to strangers who cut my raw skin and
Bound my body with the roots and fallen leaves
Noemi, a side of heaven above the salty waves of sea
I never ask you to understand me because I will miss you

My Beloved Is

My beloved is all the beats to my heart
And the breathe that makes me confident

My beloved is the colours of rainbow
And the colours of autumn leaves in heaven

My beloved is the sweet dreams and
The right path of every journey I walk above

My beloved is the bullet that awaken
Me from drinking tears and smoking down

My beloved is the sun that never sets
And the naked moon to warm my hairy chest

My beloved is the woman that cannot
Be compared to any other woman I met before

My beloved is the tears that I weep
Only if she will accept me the way I am

My beloved is the queen without a slave
And the princess on the top of a lusty mountain

My beloved is the drink that makes me
Drunk for a single night and a great kisser

My beloved is the dawn and the devil to
Tie me down in the time of real sensation

My beloved is the tree and the branch
That hides me from the winter snow

My beloved is the drops of rain that
Dance by me to the seeds and flowers

My beloved is the delicious rose
And her nightly sweats are my favourite cloud

My beloved is the scent of motherhood
And homesickness that offers me a new land

My beloved is the spirit that never betrays
And the heart that never breaks me to misery

My beloved is the colour of an angel
And has eyes of glistening snow

My beloved is not the number to count
Nor a body to describe erotically to my friends

My beloved is a lifetime yearnings
And emotions and feelings that cannot be mute

My beloved is the intense love and
The kiss that I will always be thirsty

My beloved is birth that never dies
And memories, moments cannot be forgotten

My beloved is the only reason I am
Strong to fight against the echo of haters

My beloved is the friendly wind that
Makes me weep until I am tiny drops of ice

My beloved is the gift from destiny
that was given me to take care of

My beloved is the reason I am growing
A few grey hairs which I love counting

My beloved is the age that never gets
Old, always positive and always a young soul

My beloved is the love that will extend
Into a family with kids, lovers, and parents

My beloved is the hope that never fades
And the wishes that never becomes bubbles

My beloved is the happiness I always want
And the grief that never arise in a second thought

My beloved is the trigger that I will pull
And shot myself to revive from under her beliefs

My beloved is next to me and dreaming,
I dare you and others to touch her soft hands

Ahmad Al-Khatat

Cold Hands

It is cold outside and I am
On my own with cold hands
By the car light and traffic
Yet, you are still on my mind

Nobody wants to hear me
People are busy with their own
Daily routine and endless problems
And I am weeping for missing you

The winds blows lots of leaves
And the autumn clouds drop rain
With lovers dance under the moonlight
While I am singing to all the stars

The street gets less busy and
Children sleep listening to grandparents, old tales
Meanwhile, I am dreaming of your perfume
And smiling from your old pictures

I prepare myself a warm cup of tea
With a few cigarettes left in the pack
I smoke and write about the days we loved
I warm my lips to recall your words

One thing keeps me stronger,
You are in paradise and it feels good to
See you beautiful without makeup nor
Tears from all the years I waited to kiss you

My Angel

My angel is my girlfriend
My girlfriend is my heaven
I love her and I hate myself
Together we are 1+1= one heart

If I touch her two hands
They will amaze me as they
melt away my stress and offer me a
Pleasurable experience like no other.

I have tested the waters until
I met with her and drank her
honey covered lips and wept with a nights
Tear that have sparkles of happiness

She is so beautiful that the
Sun rises and sets and I am
Unable to feel her flesh on me
Since she is my morning butterfly

A Leaf to Your Branch...

Inspire by the Titanic movie 1997

I will be always your Jack Dawson
Even if there are hundreds of men
With diamonds and roses for you
I will give my heart and spirit for you

The sun shines and sets and the moon appears
Then fades away when the sun rises.
The warm sun dies and the sky gets darker
I will be the last autumn leaf to your branch

Even when there is no tree but your seed
With a heavenly scent that once I inhale
I die from being aroused but once I
remember your kindness I am reborn

O my eyes it is late to stay awake
Isn't it time to sleep and rest?
But why should I sleep with tears
When I have nobody to wake up for

Sleep Well

Sleep well my princess
It was a long day
Close your eyes and wait for my arrival
To become the knight of your dreams

If I thought for just one moment
To tell you that I will always love you
The darkness is arising in minutes
While you are kissing me

My emotions are blossoming
between your warm heart right now
Open your arms like a flying dove
Till I catch you to fly higher together

Do not be naughty at three in the morning
Let me kiss somewhere other than your lips
Let me touch somewhere other than your breasts
Just sleep and rest well on my favourite pillow

Ahmad Al-Khatat

We Are One…

I was born
In a heartless
And careless
Homeland
Which explains
why I am a lost coin

Who is lucky
You or I ?
We love
And
Support
Each other

Till we both
Die in years,
Our relationship
Is stronger
And deeper
Than anything

Tonight
I'll be a guest
In your dreams
Just like
You will be an angel
In my prayer

The moon is cold
and I am cold, but
warm when I touch
your beautiful hands

The stars are away
The clouds are near
I stay awake looking
at your midnight eyes
Love is warm inside of
you, it feels like there is
no space for unhealthy
temptation, but there is
a sun rise…

out
of
27
letters,
I
spelled
my
love
to
you
in
more
than
27
languages

God's Whiskey

God's whiskey tastes like your lips.
pour me some before the snow covers
your elixir above the damages I caused
myself from a moment of happiness
What good is left in my past world?
I feel my wounds are nostalgic to
The times I would weep from
sorrows of losing my homeland.
You are the most beautiful prayer in my heart
You are the holiest woman between all the
-ones I have met with in past seasons
your prayer is the only season that shines
Walking to you barefoot is not a foolish dream
All the lovebirds open their cages to help me
All the people who are romantic are following me
just because you are the truest love of my life
The lord is watching me again, as I grow weaker
-drunk, from drinking more than I should responsibly
-that is why my body is bleeding rusty blood.
medicine does not cure me as much as your lips
If you come home on Christmas, I will no
longer flip open the photo albums and shed
widow tears, the passion is fed from your
fantasies, where we feel free to be in a pure love

Lips of an Angel

Lips of an angel,
they do not lie
but when they
are in sync with
mine, I adore
-their pure sugar,
their fancy wine
and their rare taste,
that will swift me
away from my life.
Kiss me before I
close my thirsty lips,
cuddle with me again
and touch my soft lips
so we can melt once more
while the night is crystal clear.
our lips are sealed waiting
for Christmas and New Year's
because between our lips
there are no conversations.
Lips of an angel are my
-untold story before my
sadness raised over my
temporary happiness, but
now I am happy that we shared
a kiss

After Twelve in the Morning

After twelve in the morning, and the
appearance of the moon and its stars,
I am thinking about you in the presence
of my silent dancing spirit with my tears.
My face becomes numb from a smile,
I share with careless and heartless people
In my heart, you are growing beautifully
In my mind, you are learning continuously
I forget my name when you wipe my sadness
but I remember that I am born for a reason
You are one of my greatest revelations, I will stab
myself if I ever hurt you, after twelve in the morning

Your Lips Are Mine

Remember, when you asked me to
-softly kiss you in the morning when
the rain was falling on your bare skin?

Put your tender lips on my dry mouth,
And steal my spirit, but do not take the fruit
away from my lonely path

My neck misses your lipstick marks lately,
I drink a lot and kiss my bottle of whiskey
just to remember that your lips are mine

The thirst for your lips does not mean
that I am looking for water, or the
spring season always walks barefoot by
the colourful flowers and butterflies

Let us cuddle tonight and break no bones,
my heart is a love letter from Christmas I
will no longer walk alone to a dry season
 just wipe my tears and I will be a love song

Sing my love poems when the music is over
 No more secrets, nor more heartbreaking or
-regrets, life is beautiful when I am resting by you,
 it feels as if love is kissing our prayers

Nobody can touch your moving lips
because you perfume is only proof
that I have kissed you in my dream

Above Your Lips

Above your lips I hear rhymes
or a love song and a love story
with a sad ending

above your lips,
little words become long haikus
and sentences become poems

above your lips I see all the colours
as a rainbow colouring my mornings,
and evenings

above your lips I observe
a unique flavour of kindness, a taste that
life has banned me in the past

above your lips the sun shines in the night
on your bare flesh, as the moon appears
when you cuddle me in your dreams.

above your lips under the stars, I will kiss your
strawberry lips, under the rain, I will marry you,
without a doubt

above your lips my tears fall,
when you play with our child and my tears fall,
when you attend my funeral

HAIKU

Noemi and I
We are the ink and a leaf
For one love letter

Ahmad Al-Khatat

our very first love letters

Ahmad Al-Khatat

DOLLARAMA

Cashier's Shift Reconciliation
Dollarama L.P. / S.E.C.

Date: ___ / ___ / ___

Instructions for this form are on the reverse side of this pad

Cashier's Name:			Float sign off:
Cash Register : #			
Env#	Time	$ Amount	Float Amount $ _____
1	: AM/PM	$	Envelope Range _____ TO _____
2	: AM/PM	$	Envelopes Used _____ TO _____
3	: AM/PM	$	Envelopes Returned _____ TO _____
4	: AM/PM	$	Envelopes Missing _____
5	: AM/PM	$	
6	: AM/PM	$	**End of Shift Register Balance** (Minus the float)
7	: AM/PM	$	
8	: AM/PM	$	Coin = $ _____
9	: AM/PM	$	_____ x $ 5 = $ _____
10	: AM/PM	$	
11	: AM/PM	$	_____ x $ 10 = $ _____
12	: AM/PM	$	_____ x $ 20 = $ _____
13	: AM/PM	$	
14	: AM/PM	$	_____ x $ 50 = $ _____
15	: AM/PM	$	_____ x $100 = $ _____
16	: AM/PM	$	
17	: AM/PM	$	_____ x $ US = $ _____
18	: AM/PM	$	
19	: AM/PM	$	End of Shift Register Balance TOTAL $ _____
20	: AM/PM	$	Envelope Balance TOTAL $ _____
21	: AM/PM	$	
22	: AM/PM	$	**End of Shift Grand TOTAL** $ _____
23	: AM/PM	$	
	Envelope Balance TOTAL	$	End of shift sign off:

VERSION 1   DOL-R.E

Noemi & Lips of Sweetness

Twenty eight years old
It feels like a funny ~~date~~
I'm so bliss for this age
Because I get to have her
in my heart, my life,
and my upcoming tomorrow
my Sexy Copsicle and mosty
the mother I have ever dreamt
for the daughter I have always loved

Smile maybe my head rests on your lips
Cry maybe my eyes weep on your cheeks
Stay strong then thatte important
So I could trust your heart to sleep next to him.

Noemi & Lips of Sweetness

> Do not let anyone claim on you because once he/she do they will die with no forgiveness from me but maybe from someone else
> I love u

Ahmad Al-Khatat was born in Baghdad, Iraq. His work has appeared in print globally and he has poems translated into several languages. He has previously been nominated for the *Best of the Net* awards. He lives in Canada.

www.ingramcontent.com/pod-product-compliance
Lightning Source LLC
Chambersburg PA
CBHW052126110526
44592CB00013B/1764